TECHNOLOGY OF THE ANCIENTS

THE
ROMANS

WIL MARA

mc Marshall Cavendish
Benchmark
New York

Other Marshall Cavendish Offices:
Marshall Cavendish International (Asia) Private Limited, 1 New Industrial Road, Singapore 536196 ● Marshall Cavendish International (Thailand) Co Ltd. 253 Asoke, 12th Flr, Sukhumvit 21 Road, Klongtoey Nua, Wattana, Bangkok 10110, Thailand ● Marshall Cavendish (Malaysia) Sdn Bhd, Times Subang, Lot 46, Subang Hi-Tech Industrial Park, Batu Tiga, 40000 Shah Alam, Selangor Darul Ehsan, Malaysia

Marshall Cavendish is a trademark of Times Publishing Limited
All websites were available and accurate when this book was sent to press.

Library of Congress Cataloging-in-Publication Data
Mara, Wil.
The Romans / Wil Mara.
p. cm. — (Technology of the ancients)
Includes bibliographical references and index.
Summary: "Focuses on the discoveries and inventions of the ancient Roman civilization in the areas of transportation, agriculture, architecture, science, and technology"—Provided by publisher.
ISBN 978-1-60870-768-3 (print) — ISBN 978-1-60870-756-0 (ebook)
1. Rome—History—Empire, 30 B.C.-476 A.D—Juvenile literature.
2. Science—Rome—History—Juvenile literature.
3. Technology—Rome—History—Juvenile literature.
4. Rome—Civilization—Juvenile literature. I. Title.
DG77.M328 2011
937—dc22
2010045269

Senior Editor: Deborah Grahame-Smith
Publisher: Michelle Bisson
Art Director: Anahid Hamparian
Series Designer: Kay Petronio

Photo research by Tracey Engel
Cover photo: Lebrecht Music and Arts Photo Library/Alamy
The photographs in this book are used by permission and through the courtesy of: *The Bridgeman Art Library*: National Museums of Scotland, 1; Look and Learn, 54. *North Wind Picture Archives*: 4, 7. *iStockphoto*: Aleksandar Vrzalski, 9; Jason Kandel, 15; Frank Romeo, 20; Michael Gray, 32. *Getty Images*: DEA/G. DAGLI ORTI, 10, 46; De Agostini, 30; Michelle Zassenhaus, 33; John W. Banagan, 36; Stephen Alvarez, 38; Christopher Furlong, 40; Stock Montage, 63. *Shutterstock*: gallimaufry, 12; Attila JÁNDI, 27. *Alamy*: Michael Jenner, 18; imagebroker, 45; The Art Gallery, 51. *Corbis*: National Geographic Society, 22. *The Art Archive*: Musée Luxembourgeois Arlon Belgium/Gianni Dagli Orti, 24; Walter Meayers Edwards/NGS Image Collection, 56.

Printed in Malaysia (T)

135642

CONTENTS

CHAPTER ONE

A CIVILIZATION FOR THE AGES

Ancient Rome was more than just a collection of people, places, and things. It was a collection of *ideas*, driven by the spirit of innovation, the thirst of curiosity, and the urge to find and create the "bigger and better" in every facet of daily life. The power and progress that shadowed the rise and fall of the Roman era represented a turning point in human history, and the influence of that period can still be felt around the world. So much of what we see and do every day bears the fingerprints of this magnificent society, its culture, and its citizens.

Just as the mightiest rivers begin with a trickle, the ascent of ancient Rome began as little more than a whisper. Sometime in the eighth century BCE, possibly in or near the year 753, a group of shepherds settled quietly on the hills of central Italy, within view of the Tiber River. These seemingly humble people carried the seeds of greatness in their hearts and minds: a

Ancient Rome was the most magnificent and progressive society of its time. Many of the advancements and luxuries we enjoy today are the direct result of the innovation and creativity of the ancient Romans.

capacity for hard work, a devotion to practicality, and a tireless ambition. They turned their tiny settlements first into bustling villages and then into dazzling cities with beautiful stone buildings, paved roadways, and lush gardens. They wrote laws, formed governments, elected leaders, and built armies. Then they reached beyond their boundaries and extended their control, as well as their citizenship, to the people of lands both near and far.

For most citizens, it was an honor to say, "I am a Roman." At its height, Rome offered a marvelously high standard of living. Home and family were vital parts of Roman life. As the head of the family, a man made most of the decisions, while a woman ran the home and watched over the children. However, Rome was also one of the first civilizations to give women increased power, which was considered outrageous in many other parts of the world. Roman women could publicly speak their minds on any subject. In later years, women ran businesses, owned land, and even played a role in government.

Education in the Roman Empire was also highly advanced— particularly starting in the second century BCE, when Rome began ruling Greece and integrated many of Greece's vast academic offerings. Children attended lessons in law, history, art, literature, spelling, math, and physical education (including combat training, for war was common during certain periods). They also learned to respect their elders, including civil authorities such as police officers and political leaders. Although formal schools were generally unavailable to the poor, children of poor families were still taught at home.

Roman political leaders took great pride in discussing important issues. They often did so in public forums, where anyone (males, mostly) could speak his mind. It was not unusual to see several people standing on

Unlike in many other ancient civilizations, women in ancient Rome were afforded many personal freedoms. They spoke their mind both at home and in public, managed businesses, and took part in political governing.

platforms in a town square, their voices booming as they tried to sway the masses to their points of view. Strong speaking skills were among the most valuable talents in society. The idea was to argue and reargue problems facing a community until a suitable solution was found.

The ancient Romans forged a government structure that continues to act as a model to this day. Leaders had advisory bodies. Ordinary citizens elected their representatives, and a system of checks and balances limited lawmakers. These were all elements of a uniquely forward-thinking people—and, perhaps most important, a people who wanted to improve the quality of everyday life.

With all this in mind, it is not surprising that ancient Rome was also an ideal environment for innovation and invention. The Romans celebrated, respected, and admired their scientists and engineers. Inventors were encouraged to come up with concepts that would improve the comfort and efficiency of daily life. When Rome became so powerful that it was looked upon as the "center of the world," many people said the Romans became arrogant and full of themselves. Perhaps this was true—but, in a strange way, it may also have helped them. A feeling of superiority may have driven Romans to create many of the advancements for which they became so famous. Surely, only the best would do in Roman society!

To think of the early Romans as inventors is not 100 percent accurate. They certainly had their share of original thoughts, but their specialty was improving upon existing ideas. Romans were known more for their practical thinking than their imaginations. Much of the technology of ancient Rome involved improvements to the ideas of the nearby civilizations of Greece and Etruria. Many of Rome's architectural successes, for example, were based directly on those of Etruscan engineers. Romans also borrowed aspects of Greek military, medical, and transportation technology and enhanced them to fit their own needs.

This does not diminish the value of what the Romans accomplished. Even if they didn't start the development of certain technologies, they moved them forward by leaps and bounds. Ancient peoples could only do so much. They didn't have many of the utilities that we take for granted today, such as electricity, oil-based fuel, and the Internet. They were also

Many structures built by the ancient Romans still stand today. This one, known simply as the Colosseum, is one of the most famous. It was the site of public events such as gladiator contests and could seat 50,000 people.

at the mercy of nature—limited by the extremes of the seasons and the rising and setting of the sun. Yet with all these constraints, Romans still accomplished great things.

The Romans left a permanent mark on the world. Through will, might, and sheer determination, they forever altered the way we live. Ancient Rome truly was a civilization for the ages.

CHAPTER TWO

GETTING AROUND THE EMPIRE

The Romans were not the first civilization to cut pathways through mountains, fields, and forests for ease of travel. Archaeological evidence shows that humans built crude roads of timber in order to pass through wetlands in present-day Europe. Stone-covered roads in the Middle East existed as far back as the fourth millennium BCE—a few thousand years before Rome even existed. By the second millennium BCE, when wheeled vehicles were playing a prominent role in human transportation throughout the Old World, people were constructing formal roadways not only to make traveling quicker and smoother, but also to prevent wear and tear on vehicles and the animals pulling them. Builders set down long planks of wood horizontally (like on a boardwalk) and held them in place with spikes or runners. The builders were careful to make the boards level to ensure as few bumps as possible. These first crude roads

The Romans were among the first to build smooth and sturdy roadways, which put less wear on their vehicles and on the animals that pulled them.

took an enormous amount of time and energy to build and served their communities for hundreds of years.

In their earliest days, the Romans used something similar to the wood-plank method. They set large, rough-hewn timbers across wetland areas in the direction they wished the road to go. Then they laid more timbers over the initial ones from left to right (again, similar to a boardwalk). They used dirt, mud, or sand to fill any openings and to keep the wood packed tight. The resulting pathways were still fairly uneven for travelers—and

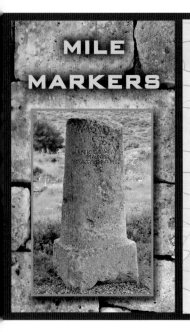

MILE MARKERS

One Roman innovation was stone markers, which stood by the roadside at regular intervals. These markers let people know the distance they had traveled, as well as the remaining distance to a certain destination. They also listed the names of towns and important landmarks. The Romans did not measure distance in miles or kilometers as we know them today. Instead, they used a unit called *milia passuum*, meaning "one thousand paces." This unit is roughly equivalent to 4,860 feet (1.5 kilometers).

they were dangerous when the logs became loose or rotted—but they were a step in the right direction.

Romans really began advancing road technology with the use of harder materials such as gravel, flagstones, and mortar. This advance grew out of their desire to provide solid, reliable, long-lasting routes for their armies. Improved transportation helped the Roman military to conquer many nearby societies and, thus, to greatly expand their empire. By the early first century CE—the time when many experts agree the Roman Empire reached its peak—Rome's power extended to all the lands touching the Mediterranean Sea. In many cases, this would not have been possible without the roads they built.

The materials and methods used in the construction of Roman roads varied tremendously. There was no set formula. Sometimes builders would lay three or four layers of material, other times just one or two. They might use mortar, concrete, or clay as a bonding agent. Sometimes there would be no bonding agent at all—builders would simply pound gravel and other small stones until they were packed tight.

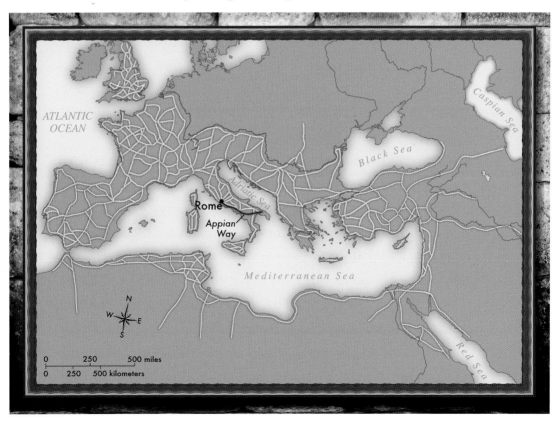

After building thousands of miles of roadways, the Romans were able to use their military might to conquer many other societies and widen their empire. The yellow lines above, which represent the actual roads, also illustrate the extent of Roman influence.

The Via Appia, better known as the Appian Way, was one of Rome's most famous routes. Its builders used clay mixed with basalt as a bonding agent. Another Roman road, built around the same period, was bonded with a mixture of gravel and lime (a white powder that is made up of calcium and oxygen). The Appian Way was outlined with square and rectangular stones called kerbstones, while the other road had a raised border made of poured concrete. One reason for all this variation was the availability of materials. Builders could only use what was around.

The first general step in building a road was deciding where to put it. Roman civil engineers tried to lay their roads as straight as possible. They had workers—usually soldiers, since the earliest roads were used for military purposes—lay down rods to outline the road's course. The next step was to dig, either by hand or with a plow. Once the trench was a few feet deep, workers filled it partially with a bedding of tough, durable material such as pebbles, sand, or gravel. Then they tamped the material down until it was tight and flat.

The road's second layer was more uniform. Builders sometimes used a larger grade of gravel. They would fill the trench until it was level with the ground. The result was a simple but effective road ready for use.

As road construction became more sophisticated, Romans often created a third layer that made the road appear more formal. They laid flagstones, cobblestones, or brick on a bed of wet mortar or concrete. Builders made roads slightly humped, so that rainwater would run to the sides rather than forming puddles and eroding the road.

There were three main types of Roman roads: *viae terrenae* (dirt roads), *viae glareatae* (improved gravel roads), and *viae munitae* (stone- or brick-paved roads).

Romans became so good at building high-quality roadways that some of them are still in use today, more than two thousand years later. Rome had a network of more than 150,000 miles (241,400 km) of roads, with some estimates running as high as 250,000 miles (402,000 km). The roads are classified as military routes (usually paved) and secondary routes for private travel (unpaved). A government administration was charged with building new roads and maintaining existing ones.

Roman roads were built so well that many not only still exist but are still usable. This one runs through a set of ruins in Jerash, Jordan. Jordan was under Roman rule until the seventh century CE.

Ironically, the same roads the Romans built in order to expand their political and economic power played a role in their downfall. By the fifth century CE, barbarians such as the Visigoths were using the roads to invade Roman cities and to attack their leaders. (The Visigoths sacked the city of Rome in 410.) In 476, the final Roman emperor, Romulus Augustulus, surrendered his rule. This effectively marked the end of more than a thousand years of Roman dominance in the region.

Romans used roads almost exclusively for business purposes—military, commercial, or political. Very rarely did people travel for pleasure. In fact,

IMPROVING ROMAN ROADS

Road construction followed the basic Roman method for many years after Rome's political collapse. In the early 1800s, a Scotsman named John Loudon McAdam carried out many experiments in the science of road building. His work resulted in the addition of drains on either side of a road, the replacement of stone foundations with ordinary soil, and the use of a new mixture of stones on the top layer. This new mix became known as "macadam" in honor of the inventor, and it is still used today.

Another common road material that has developed since Roman times is asphalt, which is mixed with gravel and other loose stones to act as a kind of concrete. This thick, dark liquid comes from petroleum and has many of the same properties as tar, such as resistance to water.

in many areas people were not allowed to travel on a Roman road without proper paperwork signed by a government official, who had to approve their reason for using the road.

Roman roads were the first to offer places where travelers could stop and rest, sleep, eat, care for their animals, and even perform basic maintenance on their carts or carriages. Usually maintained by the Roman government, rest stops were often spaced about 35 miles (56 km) apart. Government officials and military men commonly used rest stops. Their formal name, *mansiones*, derives from the Latin phrase meaning "to stay." Similar to today's way stations, the mansiones appeared to have individual reputations. For example, some were known for their comfort and good service, while others were not. Small villages and towns often built up around particularly busy and popular mansiones.

BRIDGES

Early Roman bridges were another significant contribution to transportation technology. Humans were building bridges well before the rise of Roman influence. Many were crudely constructed, however, and could not be expected to last long. One example was a bridge built in the thirteenth century BCE in an area of modern-day Turkey known as Hattusas. Spanning just over 20 feet (6 meters), it was made of rough timber and had piles of stone on either side of the river to act as supports. For many centuries wood was the most common material used in bridge making, as it was readily available and easy to work with.

The Romans built their earliest bridges with wood as well. By about the second century BCE, however, they began using stronger materials, such as large stones held together with concrete. They also utilized a relatively new and important design feature: the arch. With its semicircular shape,

Ancient Roman engineers were the first to make extensive use of the arch. The arch's greatest value came from its ability to disperse the forces of stress, thus making any structure considerably more durable.

an arch could withstand great amounts of stress because it dispersed the force of whatever weight was on top of it. This made arches perfect for the needs of a bridge. The Romans were not the first people to discover an arch's strength; the nearby Etruscan society, which Rome eventually absorbed into its own, had been using arches for years. The Romans adopted the arch and then expanded its usefulness.

Because the purpose of a bridge is often to continue a route across a body of water or a valley, bridge building can be considered an extension of road building. And as they did with roadways, Romans built bridges with both solidity and longevity in mind. Roman engineers did not want to have to repair their bridges constantly.

Building a bridge across a moving body of water, rather than a dry valley, was a challenge for Roman engineers. The first step involved setting down the foundation. Sometimes this required the builders to ram heavy timbers into the riverbed to act as pilings. Later on, however, they would set watertight walls in the river to redirect its flow and then lay foundations of stone in the open space left behind. Stone foundations had much greater strength than wooden pilings. Roman engineers faced another challenge if the land on either side of a river or valley fell away at too sharp of an angle. To solve this, the builders might first have to add more earth or building material so a traveler would not experience a dip when approaching the bridge.

Builders created arches with the help of trusses—supports that kept the stones in place until they could stand on their own. Workers laid additional stones between the arches to create a top span. They then built walls on either side of the span to keep travelers safe. Early on, builders used mortar to hold all the materials together, but the Romans eventually began using a powerful form of concrete that they discovered. Some of the later Roman bridges were made of bricks instead of stones.

As Roman engineers became more comfortable building stone-and-concrete bridges, they discovered ways to improve the design. For example, they created oval-shaped bases so that water would flow more easily around them. Engineers also began to put holes in the bases so that water could flow through rather than constantly pounding against the surface. Some Roman bridges had one long arch rather than several smaller ones. This was likely because it was easier to build an arch from

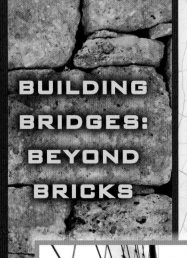

BUILDING BRIDGES: BEYOND BRICKS

Arched bridges remained standard for many centuries. As most Roman bridges stayed in excellent condition, engineers around the world continued to copy the designs. By the eighteenth century, however, iron began to overshadow stones and concrete. Iron was inexpensive and more pliable than earlier materials, which meant builders could bend and shape it as needed. By the early 1800s, almost all new bridges were being made from iron.

The next major step in bridge building occurred in the mid- to late 1800s, when people developed an even better metal called steel by mixing iron and carbon. (The famous Brooklyn Bridge in New York City, built in 1869, is made of steel.) Steel was both stronger and lighter than iron. Today, engineers are developing different types of cable-stay bridges, which can span huge areas. In this type of bridge, cables leading from tall columns are attached to the bridge deck at regular intervals. Both steel and concrete can be used in different parts of the cable-stay design.

one shoreline to another than to set a foundation in the water. A few Roman bridges looked a bit strange in that some of the arches were wider than others. This happened because the builders couldn't find enough solid spots in the riverbed to set the foundations evenly.

One feature that set Roman bridges apart from those of other cultures was their size. The span between arches could be anywhere from 15 to 60 feet (4.6 to 18.3 m), which made some spans enormous for the period. One of the longest Roman-built bridges, located in Spain, reached nearly 2,575 feet (785 m)—an incredible achievement. A few bridges also had beautiful carvings and relief accents, often cast in colorful marble. This was rare, however, as marble was both heavy and expensive, and the artwork took extra time and labor. Such a bridge was likely built for the exclusive use of government leaders.

CHAPTER THREE

THE FARMER'S LIFE

Running a farm in ancient Rome required a great deal of manual labor, meaning farmers had to work with their hands. The days could be very long, and the hard work took a severe toll on the body. Romans of the lower social classes, however, did not have the skills to do much else.

Harvesting grain—the process of removing the seeded heads from the stalks—was tedious and time consuming when done manually. The grain was ready for harvesting when the head of the stalk took on a bushy texture and a golden color. The worker had to cut the stalks with a scythe as close to the ground as possible and then tie them into bundles. The cut stalks had to sit for a time until they were fully dried out. Then farmers had to thresh the stalks—beat the heads until all the seeds came out. Finally, they winnowed the grain. This meant separating the seeds from all the unwanted material that came out during threshing.

As the population of ancient Rome grew, so did the need for agricultural products. In the earliest days, farmwork was done by hand—which was exhausting. Over time, however, the Romans made several advancements in farming technology.

Harvesting required a large number of workers. A good-sized field might take a day or more to clear. As Rome grew, so did its population—and the demand for food. Since grain was a staple item, the increasing demand soon resulted in shortages. In many areas, there was plenty of grain, but it was taking too long to harvest and process it.

During the first century CE, in an area known as Gaul (located in the northwestern part of the Roman Empire), farmers developed a device that greatly increased the efficiency of the grain-harvesting chore. It was a simple but cleverly designed reaper, which the Romans called a vallus. Based on the few ancient images that remain from this period, the vallus looks similar to a wheelbarrow, except that it had a row of sharp, comblike teeth jutting out from the front. The handles extended back much farther then a wheelbarrow and then turned inward until they met to create an enclosure. Farmers strapped a donkey or ox to the inside of the vallus to move it along. A worker stood behind the animal to lift the front of the vallus higher or lower depending on the height of the grain stalks.

As the vallus rolled forward, the heads of the stalks broke off and fell into the boxlike tray. The teeth at the front had upturned

Roman farmers developed a device called a vallus, which made it much easier to harvest grain. A field that would take days to reap could be cleared in a matter of hours.

tips, which helped to scoop the falling heads while minimizing loss of grain. Because the edges of the tray were wider at the front than at the back, stalks that might have become wrapped around the vallus's axles were pushed aside. Sometimes a second worker walked along with a stick and cleared out the teeth if they became clogged. In spite of all these precautions, farmers still lost some grain when they used the vallus. The machine's wheels, the animal's hooves, and the workers' feet sometimes crushed stalks that were particularly short.

The development of the vallus increased the volume of grain that Roman farmers could harvest each season. A field that might take a team of workers several days to clear could be finished in one day with the help of a vallus. With two or three valluses, the work might take mere hours. Considering that the harvesting season in Gaul was relatively brief, and there was a chronic shortage of workers, the vallus was a major step forward.

Ironically, the vallus never became very popular in Rome outside Gaul. Farmers used it less and less until the device was forgotten entirely. Some historians believe this happened because Roman leaders feared that farm laborers would stage an uprising when they lost their jobs due to the vallus's efficiency. Ironically, a device very similar to the reaper may have been used in China in the fourteenth century—and then abandoned for the exact same reason.

WATER MILLS

A water mill is a group of structures that use water to power a milling device. One of these structures is usually a waterwheel—a large wheel that turns as it interacts with moving or falling water. The ultimate purpose of a mill is to break large pieces of a material into smaller pieces. Ancient

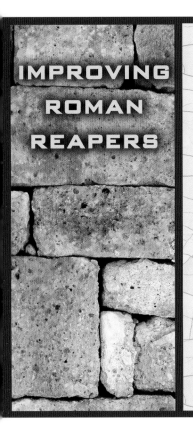

IMPROVING ROMAN REAPERS

In the mid-1800s, an inventor named John Ridley saw a drawing of a Roman reaper in a book called *Encyclopaedia of Agriculture*. Ridley decided to introduce the machine to the modern world. Around the same time, American farmer and inventor Cyrus Hall McCormick developed a horse-drawn reaper, which he patented in 1834. In the early 1910s, the International Harvester Company developed a machine that both harvested and threshed grain. Today, harvesting machines perform all three important tasks—reaping, threshing, and cleaning—as they move through fields and leave waste matter behind. There are different types of harvesters for different types of crops. The work these machines can perform in hours would have taken a team of laborers many weeks in Roman times.

Romans used mills to grind foods such as wheat and other grains into a meal or fine flour. Later on, the Romans found other uses for mills.

The construction of a basic water mill was fairly simple. The builder set the lower portion of a large waterwheel into a moving body of water. A series of scoops or paddles, which ran along the outside of the waterwheel, caught the water. Attached to the center of the waterwheel was a long pole called an axle. The other end of the axle ran into a small building. Inside the building, the axle first went through the center of a stationary circular stone and then connected with a second circular stone that moved. As the water spun the waterwheel outside, the second circular stone also spun. Any grain set between the two stone wheels would be ground into meal or flour.

The ancient Romans were not the first to build water mills; Greeks were using them long before the rise of Roman influence. Several design problems limited the mills' effectiveness, however. At first the waterwheels were set horizontally in the water. This meant the wheels could only move as fast as the water flowed—and this was a problem if a river or stream dried up. Also, for the wheel to be truly effective, the water had to be flowing fairly rapidly.

The Romans made several design changes that drastically improved the usefulness of the water mill. First, they switched the position of the waterwheel from horizontal to vertical. While this increased

The Romans were not the first to make use of the power of flowing water via waterwheels—it was an idea they took from the Greeks. However, they did make some notable improvements. They turned the wheels upright (vertical) and then built dams downstream to control the water's flow.

the waterwheel's turning ability, it meant the waterwheel's axle could no longer directly connect to the two mill wheels, which had to remain horizontal so that mill workers could use them. Thus, mill builders had to install a pair of gears—one at the end of the waterwheel's axle, the other at the end of the mill wheel's axle. When the gears were connected, the waterwheel axle could once again turn the mill wheel axle.

The Romans' second major innovation was to change the waterwheel from undershot to overshot. This meant the flow of water would fall onto the waterwheel from above rather than run underneath it. Builders accomplished this by piling dirt and stones into the streambed or created raised chutes through which the water would flow. Once scoops or buckets were fitted onto the wheel, they would fill with water as the wheel turned and then empty back into the stream when they reached the bottom. The force of gravity from the falling water greatly increased the power generated by the waterwheel.

Romans took this new setup a step further when they discovered they could control the flow of water by building dams a short distance behind the spot where the water reached the wheel. This caused the river water to accumulate in an area that became known as a millpond. The dam had doors that could be opened or closed as needed, and the water flowed down chutes set at sharp angles to increase the speed and force. Whereas an older mill might be able to produce about 15 pounds (6.8 kilograms) of flour per hour, the new Roman water mill could make twenty times as much in the same amount of time.

It wasn't long before the Romans began expanding upon this system to achieve even greater results. Production increased tremendously when they made the wheel larger or wider, or when they used more than one. In areas where the water could be manipulated to flow in powerful rushes,

Another step in the evolution of the Roman water mill was the development of the floating mill. When Romans became the target of frequent attacks by neighboring nations toward the end of their rule, they often found their water supplies cut off or their mills destroyed. The demand for flour and related products was still just as high, however. So builders created a mill by setting a waterwheel between two boats, which they then anchored in place in a fast-moving river. The mill wheels were located in the boats, where corn could be ground as the river's current turned the waterwheel. While the floating water mill may have been more cumbersome to operate, it supplied tons of much-needed food to Roman citizens during a difficult time.

THE FLOATING MILL

workers would build several mills, with as many as a dozen wheels going at a time. Such mills could turn out flour by the ton—some estimates are as high as 25 to 30 tons per day—while just a few pounds per hour had been considered impressive previously.

For many centuries, people around the world continued to use waterwheels based largely on Roman design but adjusted to fit individual needs. In parts of Africa, central Asia, and the Middle East, waterwheels powered mills that produced everything from paper and sugar to rice and steel. Steel became the material of choice for the construction of waterwheels after engineers discovered that this lighter, tougher material would turn faster than wood, thus increasing the wheel's effectiveness. The demise of the waterwheel began in the 1700s with the development of the turbine, a device that turns the power of moving water into mechanical energy such as electricity.

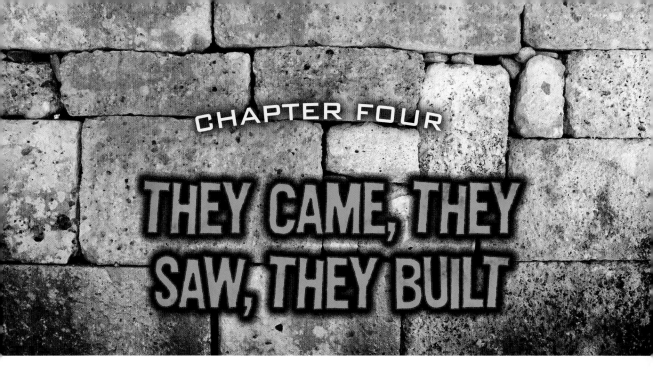

CHAPTER FOUR

THEY CAME, THEY SAW, THEY BUILT

Concrete is a hard construction material that is formed by mixing cement, bits of other solid material (such as gravel or sand), and water. When the proper amounts of each element are combined, the water is absorbed and the other elements harden to form a material that is stonelike in toughness and density. Since many different types of material can be used, the term *concrete* is fairly general. Builders use concrete for everything from roads and bridges to walls and underground pipes. The strongest types of concrete, which are water resistant and long lasting, are ideal for building.

Ancient peoples were using primitive forms of concrete thousands of years before the Romans did. A mixture of small stones, mud, and straw formed a simple kind of concrete when it dried. Archaeologists have found evidence of simple concretes used in the area of modern-day Serbia and Montenegro around 5600 BCE, and the ancient Egyptians may have been

The Romans were not the first society to use concrete, but they were the first to make it using a volcanic ash called pozzolana. Pozzolana concrete became the hardest and strongest of its time.

building with the material around 3000 BCE. The Greeks mixed limestone, rubble, and various clays into their concrete shortly before the Romans began using it.

The Romans were lucky in that they had a wide selection of materials to mix into concrete. Over the centuries, Roman builders experimented with various sands, ashes, stones, and clays. The region's rich volcanic activity left behind a wealth of geological goodies to choose from. It is likely that some of the builders' success was simply lucky, as they could only use what was lying within a reasonable distance. It is also likely, then, that pure luck led them to discover what turned out to be the best possible material for concrete production: a volcanic ash called pozzolana. Pozzolanic ash is very fine, like sand, and is found in four basic colors—black, gray, white, and brick red.

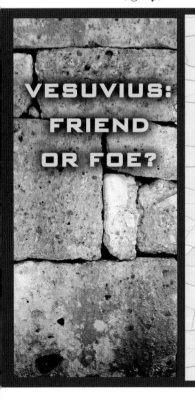

VESUVIUS: FRIEND OR FOE?

Pozzolana gets its name from the location of its initial discovery: Pozzuoli, part of the Naples province. Vesuvius is the volcano that produced the bulk of pozzolana ash in that area. There is some irony here, as Mount Vesuvius, while providing the Romans with the perfect concrete-making material, also killed more than a thousand people and buried several Roman cities when it erupted in 79 CE.

Romans took great pride in their architecture, and many elements of their design work are still widely used in architecture today. This structure, the famous Pantheon, features the ornate columns familiar to the Roman style.

Pozzolana makes such a good element in concrete because of the way it reacts when mixed with powdered lime and water. Once combined, the resulting concrete is incredibly strong. At the time of pozzolana's discovery, no other material came even close to its bonding abilities. The Romans realized that pozzolana was water resistant, so they could use it to build foundations for structures that would be set in rivers, lakes, and seas. Pozzolana concrete also showed a strong resistance to flaking, which made it extra long lasting.

Since other forms of concrete had caused disappointments in the past, Roman builders were at first suspicious of pozzolana, so they used it sparingly. By the first century CE, they used it as mortar when constructing foundations and low-income housing tenements. What may have swayed the attention of Roman engineers was the discovery that pozzolana was also fireproof. In 64 CE, the Great Fire of Rome killed thousands of Roman citizens and destroyed ten of Rome's fourteen districts—but materials made with pozzolana remained standing. After the fire, builders used bricks and pozzolana concrete in most construction projects.

As the years passed and Roman builders became more confident in the pozzolana mixture, they began using it to create some of their most stunning architecture. A good example, and one of the most beautiful of all Roman sites, is the Pantheon. Originally intended as a place of worship to Roman gods, the building features massive stone columns more than 40 feet (12 m) high, bronze doors that once were gold plated, and a rotunda with a concrete dome that weighs more than 5,000 tons (4,536 metric tons). The only source of light is the wide hole at the dome's peak—an incredible feat of engineering in itself. Nearly two thousand years later, the Pantheon stands as a shining testament not only to the ingenuity of Roman builders, but also to the awesome power of pozzolana concrete. The building, which is still used today, remains in excellent condition.

AQUEDUCTS

From the beginning of time, humans have needed clean freshwater. In the earliest days, people got water from wherever it was most readily available—streams, lakes, rivers, and so on. They also used buckets and

Little has changed in the use and composition of concrete since Roman times. In 1824, however, a bricklayer named Joseph Aspdin patented a Portland cement, which is similar to the Romans' pozzolana cement and is now used worldwide. His son, William, later added the mineral alite to his father's mixture. This improvement enabled the Portland cement to strengthen before it hardened completely—a characteristic that made it a much more desirable construction material. Today there are several varieties of Portland cement, as well as non-Portland varieties designed for specialized purposes.

CONCRETE SINCE ROMAN TIMES

barrels to collect water during rainstorms. People could store water in large containers for later use, which was particularly important during seasons when streams dried up and storms were few and far between. In short, water was a crucial element of everyday life, and running out of it put a person in dire circumstances.

The Romans were not the first ancient civilization to utilize the concept of an aqueduct—a channel built for the purpose of moving large quantities of water from one place to another. People in Assyria, Egypt, India, Persia (Iran), and other places were using primitive aqueducts long before the rise of Rome. But Roman engineers, ever brilliant and innovative, made huge strides in the design and effectiveness of aqueducts. Many aqueduct principles of Roman invention are used to this day.

What drove the need for the Romans to create a network of aqueducts (as well to build large and magnificent cities) was likely the population explosion that resulted from significant improvements in trade and agriculture. With so many people coming to Rome to be part of the empire's great society, the old methods of acquiring water simply wouldn't do. Roman leaders realized they needed a steady flow of drinkable water from a source that would probably never run out. Since some of these sources were miles away, Roman engineers had their work cut out for them.

Romans began building the first of many major aqueducts in the late fourth century BCE. (The earliest known aqueduct was built in 312.) The first step was to find a suitable source of water. In most cases the source was located high in the hills or mountains surrounding a city. Then engineers

Most of an aqueduct's run was located underground, but some sections had to be built above ground. Handsomely rendered using the familiar arch design, these sections were called arcades.

would have to decide how to channel the water from its source to the city. They used one of three channeling methods: tunnels bored right through solid rock, aboveground stone-and-mortar tunnels, and arcades—open troughs supported by arches. Any of the three channels could be lined with hard, waterproof cement.

The general rule for an aqueduct was that the water had to flow down into the city at a reasonable pace. That meant the downward tilt of the aqueduct had to be very slight. For example, most aqueducts had a tilt of no more than 0.14 percent, resulting in a fall of about 6 inches (15 centimeters) for every 100 feet (30 m). If the tilt was too severe, the water would flow too quickly and eventually wear out the channel—and aqueducts were too expensive and time consuming to build for that. The challenge of keeping the tilt slight sometimes meant that the route of the aqueduct had to snake and wind around in strange directions. In places where engineers felt the water was still moving too fast, they might place obstructions in the flow to slow it down.

The main bulk of the average aqueduct was set underground, either in the form of a tunnel bored through solid rock or as piping. If the rock was permeable—meaning that water could seep through it—builders would line the rock with clay or concrete. Sometimes they would make holes in the underground channels to permit air ventilation or access if someone needed to perform maintenance. Some aqueducts had the additional feature of an occasional sedimentation tank, which filtered out junk that floated in the water. Some aqueducts even had a second flow of water in case one had to be shut down in case of an emergency.

The most visually stunning segments of any aqueducts are probably the arcades. These are the parts of the aqueduct where the water flow is literally lifted off the ground. The channel through which the water moves is set upon a series of arches similar to those of bridges and other structures. Although many photographs of Roman aqueducts draw attention to the arcades, these structures made up only a small percentage of aqueduct routes.

Aqueducts took a lot of time, effort, and money to build, so Roman engineers used them only when absolutely necessary. The structures' main purpose was to bring the water flow to such a height that it would build up a bit more speed before finally spilling into a large tank called a cistern, located in the city where the water would be used. Builders also used arcades if the aqueduct's route hit a low spot, such as a valley, and the engineers wanted to keep the flow of water above it. The tallest Roman-built arcade, located in Spain, was more than 150 feet (46 m) above the

In order for water to flow through an aqueduct, the duct had to be tilted at a very slight angle—just enough to cause the water to flow, but not too swiftly. Usually the duct was pitched at an angle of less than 1 percent, which amounted to a drop of about 6 inches (15 cm) for every 100 feet (30 m).

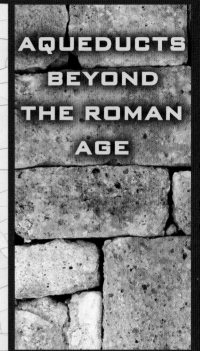

The basic principles of aqueducts have changed little since Roman times, and a few of the ancient aqueducts still channel water to towns, cities, and industrial sites. We still take water from large sources and channel it into towns, cities, and industrial sites. Most aqueducts are underground to keep the water well protected, and some take the water from naturally occurring underground sources called aquifers. The pipes used in today's aqueducts have improved since the Roman days. Instead of boring simple tunnels through rock, we use modern materials such as PVC (a tough, durable plastic). Aqueducts are also longer than ever; some reach hundreds of miles in length.

AQUEDUCTS BEYOND THE ROMAN AGE

ground. Most arcades were much smaller than that. Engineers kept them low so they could be easily inspected and repaired.

The cisterns were not the final destination for water after it zoomed through the aqueducts. Water then traveled through pipes or troughs to private homes throughout the city. Government leaders and wealthy residents received a direct flow. Other people often had to bring buckets to collect water from large fountains. Aqueducts also fed water into public baths, pools, and industrial sites such as mines, mills, and forges. Experts estimate that a total of 260 miles (418 km) of aqueducts were built during the third and second centuries BCE to serve Rome itself, and hundreds more were built for other areas under Roman control.

The fall of Rome, which began in the late third to early second century CE, coincided with the decline of the aqueducts. As people began leaving Rome's cities, the demand for freshwater decreased. When enemy soldiers began to attack the Roman Empire, one of their primary targets was the aqueducts, as cutting off water supplies was a quick and effective way to bring a society to ruin.

HYPOCAUSTS

The idea of keeping an entire room warm through a central source of heat has existed in one form or another for ages. The discovery of fire led to the earliest heat sources. In a way, the concept of lighting and maintaining a small fire in a cave was similar to a central heating system. As humans became more sophisticated, so did their methods of heating interior spaces. The Greeks, for example, discovered that they could warm rooms from underneath by digging tunnels under their homes and filling the tunnels with hot air provided by outside fires. They called this approach

Hypocausts provided heating in a Roman home through ducts in the flooring, through which heat from a fire was channeled. This was an expensive setup, however, and usually only seen in the homes of the wealthiest citizens.

a hypocaust, which came from the Greek word *hypokauston* (in Latin, *hypocaustum*)—"burning (or heating) from below."

The Romans took the hypocaust several steps further by improving its efficiency and expanding its uses. First they created tunnels of a sort underneath floors by excavating a hole, laying the foundation (which had a hole for channeling heat), and building a series of small pillars a few feet apart. They built a floor upon the pillars and then added a second, more decorative, layer of flooring. A fire burning outside (or in a small, well-ventilated chamber) acted as a small furnace, and the heat flowed through ducts until it filled the area under the flooring. Small holes under the floor directed heat to the roof through tubes in the walls in order to release excess heat, smoke, and soot.

Hypocausts did not make it into every Roman home. They were expensive to build and even more expensive to maintain. To keep the heat flowing, someone had to feed wood—or any other spare material that would burn—into the fire constantly. Servants or slaves played this role, but not everyone could afford to have such a person on hand. Hypocausts were usually found in one of two locations—homes of the well-to-do and public bathhouses.

Hypocaust systems in public bathhouses often had a second feature—a water element. Water was stored in large metal tanks above the fire and piped into different rooms of the bathhouse. In one room, the steam might come up through the floor and create a simple but effective sauna. In another, it might heat a small pool and provide an ancient hot tub. Public baths had rooms of different temperatures. The warmest room, also known as the *caldarium*, was closest to the furnace. The next warmest room was called the *tepidarium* (which was lukewarm), followed by the *frigidarium* (which could be quite cool).

By the early 1700s, engineers (possibly Russian) began feeding hot water, rather than heated air, through hypocaust pipes, and in the mid-nineteenth century people were using steam. Today the pipe system is used almost exclusively in homes and other buildings, and the source of heat can be anything from electricity to oil. Today's furnaces are smaller and more efficient than ever. Gone are the days of having to feed wood into the flames to keep the heat constant.

While the Romans improved the original Greek idea of the hypocaust, they may have overlooked one important problem: carbon monoxide poisoning. Carbon monoxide gas is produced when organic items burn in areas with poor ventilation. Since the gas has no smell or taste, it would have been impossible for the Romans to know it was even present. Some experts believe carbon monoxide poisoning caused serious illness in Romans who either used hypocausts too frequently or spent time in areas that lacked adequate ventilation.

INSULAE

While the wealthiest Romans lived in comfortable homes, complete with their own sources of water and heat as well as private gardens and beautiful art, those on the poorer end of the Roman society often had to live in crudely built apartment buildings known as insulae. The Latin word *insula* means "island." Some historians believe this name describes the bird's-eye view of the many insulae that stood around Rome and its major cities—from above, they must have looked like islands. The Romans were the first to provide housing for their citizens in this manner. They were, in this sense, the first formal apartment blocks.

In spite of the ingenuity and occasional brilliance of Roman engineers, insulae were anything but architectural marvels. First and foremost, they were frightfully unsafe. They were usually built with the cheapest materials and the quickest methods. Many insula landlords, driven by greed, did not want to spend a lot of time and money on construction. Most insulae, for example, were made of cheap materials instead of high-quality pozzolana cement. As a result, the two greatest risks to an insula resident were fire and structural collapse. In fact, it is a matter of record that insulae either went up in flames or tumbled into piles of rubble all the time—and usually killed the occupants in the process.

Nevertheless, residents of insulae willingly paid their rents and accepted the risks. Even if you were poor, you had to live somewhere. Small-time business owners were also attracted to insulae because landlords reserved the first floor for shops rather than living quarters. Ironically, the lower levels were the safest. Upper floors were built quickly and sloppily, and they were often so small that they could barely be considered living spaces. Occasionally they were not even made from bricks or cement, but from timber. Risk of fire or collapse was therefore even greater.

There were other problems associated with living in insulae. They rarely had running water, so residents had to fetch water from a public fountain. Very few insulae had bathrooms, so tenants had to use public latrines. An apartment resident living on an upper floor might relieve himself in a bucket several times over the course of a few days and then carry the bucket down several flights of stairs before emptying it at a

INSIDE TODAY'S INSULAE

Since Roman times, apartment buildings have remained popular as a way of living relatively inexpensively without being burdened by the upkeep of a home and the land on which it sits. In the tenth century BCE, Egyptians began building impressive apartments, some of them more than a dozen stories high. Some apartments in the Yemeni city of Shibam were as tall as 130 feet (40 m), which was unusual for the time. The most dramatic improvements to apartments since ancient times have involved their construction. Some nations now have strict building rules to ensure the safety of all occupants. There are elevators as well as stairwells in case of fire. Concrete walls are reinforced with steel, and thick steel beams run horizontally under the floors. Architects know all the greatest stress points, so they build certain areas of an apartment building stronger than others. In this way, the building is safer and lasts longer. Modern engineers also have the benefit of new technology—such as computers, which can create excellent simulations—to help them foresee structural problems. The ancient Romans had none of these advantages.

Ancients Romans did not observe quite the same degree of privacy in their public toilets that we do today. It is also unpleasant to imagine what an urgent visit here would have been like in cold weather.

public waste-disposal site. Sometimes tenants would get fed up and simply dump the bucket's contents out an open window.

Insula windows did not have glass until around the second century CE. Prior to that, windows were usually nothing more than openings in the wall. During times of harsh weather, tenants would have to find a way to block the openings. In warmer seasons, they could cover windows with a curtain or a blanket. Nevertheless, it was hard to sleep with all the noise coming from below. The sounds were enough to keep anyone awake—businessmen haggling with customers, children playing to blacksmiths hammering on anvils, carts rattling down cobbled streets, and more.

MENSIS
OCTOBER
DIES·XXXI
NONAE
SEPTIMAN
DIES
HOR·X S·
NOX
HOR·XIIII·
SOL
LIBRA
TVTELA
MARTIS
VINDEMIAE

MENSIS
NOVEMBER
DIES·XXX
NON·QVINT
DIES·HOR·VIIII·S
NOX·IT·OR·XIIII·S
SOL
SCORPIONE
TVTELA
DEANAE
SEMENTES
TRITICARIAE
ET·HORDIAR
SCROBATIO
ARBORVM
IOVIS

MENSIS
DECEMB
DIES·XXXI
NON·QVINT
DIES·HOR·VIIII
NOX·HOR·XV
SOL·SAGITT
TVTEL·VESTAE
HEMPS·NITIV
SIVE·TROPAE
CHIMERIN
VINEAS·STERC
FABA·SERINES
MATERIAS
DEICIENTES
OLIVA·LEGENT

CHAPTER FIVE

DEVICES FOR EVERYDAY LIFE—AND DEATH

The Romans, like many people before them, wanted to devise a system for keeping track of the days, months, and years. The earliest Romans probably borrowed their calendar system from the Greeks. The Greek system was based on the phases of the moon rather than the movement of the sun, which guides the calendar we use today. The Romans made three major changes to their calendar before the fall of the empire in 476.

The moon goes through a full cycle of phases in 29 days, 12 hours, and 44 minutes. The Romans observed these phases much like we do today—simply by looking at the night sky. In each phase, a different part of the moon is visible (except in a new moon phase, when it is entirely dark). The light that shines on the moon comes from the sun. Since the sun and moon are in different positions each night, only certain parts of the moon are "lit." Imagine shining a flashlight onto a tennis ball in a dark room. If you move the flashlight around, you will only be able to see certain parts of the ball.

One of the most important changes the Romans made to the calendar was to base it on the movement of the sun rather than the phases of the moon.

The first Roman calendar was divided into three parts. The first part was called the kalends (or calends). The kalends, which followed the first crescent moon after the new moon, was considered the beginning of a new month. The next part was called the nones, which began with the half moon and occurred on the fifth or seventh day of the month. Finally, the ides came on the night of the full moon—either the thirteenth or the fifteenth day of the month. At this point in the calendar's evolution, there were no days of the week. The Romans just had a kind of countdown to the start of the next kalends, nones, or ides.

In Roman society, a man called a pontifex or pontiff, usually a priest, watched for the changes in moon phases and informed his community where they were in the calendar. He also told his fellow citizens how many days it would be until the next change occurred.

The problem with the early Roman calendar was that it had only ten months, for a total of 304 days in a year. This, of course, did not match the true yearly cycle of the sun, so the Romans ended up with about sixty-one "leftover" days each year. Their solution to this issue was essentially to ignore the extra days, by letting them pass during the winter months when there was no farming activity. Still, it was clear that the calendar needed some improvements.

WHAT'S IN A NAME?

It is not a coincidence that the word *kalends* is so similar to *calendar*. The word refers to the job of the pontifex, as it comes from the Latin *calare*, which means "to call out." The modern months of July and August are named after Julius and Augustus Caesar. These months' original names were Quinctilis and Sextilis.

The first person to make these improvements was Numa Pompilius, one of Rome's earliest leaders. Sometime around 700 BCE, Pompilius added two months to the beginning of the calendar in order to bring it closer to the solar year. The new months were called Januarius (later called January) and Februarius (February). Pompilius's additions fleshed out the calendar to a new total of 355 days.

This still left the Romans a few days short of a true solar year, but it was harder to notice now. The solution this time was to add another month, called Mercedonius, every two years to make up the difference. This caused some headaches because the addition of Mercedonius didn't occur on a regular basis. The Romans sometimes failed to include it when they really should have, which made the new calendar system a bit of a mess. But at least they were getting closer.

Finally, the famous Roman leader Julius Caesar came along in 46 BCE and ordered that the calendar be reworked once again. He decided that, starting in 45 BCE, the calendar would follow the solar year rather than the phases of the moon, and it would have 365 days. An astronomer named Sosigenes of Alexandria told Caesar that the solar year actually lasted 365.25 days. This seemed like a problem, since it would be impossible to observe a quarter of a day. So Caesar decided to add an extra day at the end of February every fourth year—thus giving birth to the concept of a leap year—to cover the difference. This final Roman calendar became known as the Julian calendar.

MEDICAL KNOWLEDGE AND EQUIPMENT

It was the Greeks, rather than the Romans, who first made large strides in the advancement of medical knowledge. Even then, the Greeks based much of their knowledge on that of the Egyptians, who were pioneers in the field much earlier. The Greeks established formal medical schools around the early fifth century BCE, and the Greek physician Hippocrates, often called the Father of Medicine, came up with treatment and care methods that we use to this day.

When the Romans began governing the Greeks in 146 BCE, they acquired many of Greece's finest doctors and medical practices. For many years afterward, Greek doctors—even though they were regarded as slaves or lowly subjects of Roman society—were charged with treating the ill.

Eventually the Romans began to develop their own ideas about health and medicine. For example, they were far more interested in preventive medicine—that is, preventing sickness in the first place—than the Greeks, who put more focus on studying an existing illness and then treating it. Driven by the preventive approach, the Romans developed hot public baths (thermae), systems for fresh-flowing water (aqueducts), food-processing and preservation methods, and an advanced sewage system.

As the Romans established an increasingly powerful military, they tried to develop medical techniques that would maintain soldiers' health. This was important because the Roman armies relied on warfare to expand their empire. It often meant Roman physicians had to treat soldiers on, or very close to, the field of battle. Since this could be very dangerous work, military leaders often lured physicians with impressive titles, generous salaries, tax breaks, and tracts of land once their term of service was over. Romans also began building their own medical schools.

As Roman armies found themselves in one battle after another for hundreds of years, and doctors treated all kinds of wounds and afflictions, the Romans' base of medical knowledge grew tremendously. Doctors were facing new challenges, such as performing on-the-spot treatments and

The Romans were likely the first society to place an emphasis on preventive medicine—that is, taking measures to prevent illnesses before they occurred. To this end, they gave special attention to everything from personal hygiene practices to effective food processing and preservation.

procedures that would have been unlikely under normal circumstances. Although many Roman soldiers still suffered, doctors were acquiring information that would save countless lives later on.

Roman physicians also began inventing various medical tools or modifying existing ones. A spatula, for example, was a double-ended, flat-headed tool. One side was used for mixing various medications, and the other was used for applying them. Doctors used long metal probes with a hooked end, sometimes called traction hooks, to open wounds for cleaning. Saws served the grisly purpose of cutting through bone, so that physicians could remove damaged fingers, toes, or entire limbs. Forceps were designed to cut away broken fragments of the skull, or to cut through the skull completely to access the brain. And bone levers—rods with

GOOD LIVING EQUALS GOOD HEALTH

The Greeks believed that the gods played a large role in a person's health. For example, if you got sick, it could be a sign that the gods were angry with you. The Romans, on the other hand, felt people's health was within their control and therefore their responsibility. The way to remain in good health, they believed, was to practice good habits and to live righteously. If you became ill, it wasn't the fault of the gods—it was yours.

slightly curved and flattened tips—were used to realign broken bones. It is interesting to note that many of these tools had household uses before Roman surgeons realized their value in medical practice. Forceps, for example, were used in cooking, and tweezers were likely part of a woman's makeup kit.

THE ART OF WAR

As the early Roman population expanded, so did its need for more land and more agricultural products. This was one of the basic driving forces behind the development of the Roman military system. In essence, the Romans found it expedient to conquer surrounding areas in order to meet their ever-increasing needs. What began as a relatively meager assemblage of unpaid and inexperienced citizenry, many of whom were farmers, evolved into the most powerful military machine of its time. At its peak, the Roman army was one of the predominant features of Roman society—so much so that a sizable portion of Roman taxes went to pay and equip the legions. The culture of the Roman military elite included harsh training techniques and an adherence to the most rigid discipline, which helped produce the most feared and fearless soldiers of their day.

Roman political strategy included more than simple military attacks. In order to undermine a rival state, Roman leaders might use subtle manipulation—for example, they might bribe foreign governments either to act in Roman interests or not to interfere with Roman affairs. Another practice was to depose or outright assassinate foreign leaders and replace them with puppet rulers controlled by Rome. The republic's military leaders considered these methods normal parts of warfare.

Roman military engineers played a crucial role in foreign campaigns, and they were far more advanced technologically than most opponents. Military engineering involves altering a battlefield environment for the purpose of giving your side a significant advantage. At the peak of Rome's military power, many soldiers carried shovels and utility knives as part of their standard traveling kit, since minor engineering tasks might be required at a moment's notice. Larger projects included building roads exclusively for military transport, erecting walls either to defend Roman forces or to contain and surround the forces of an enemy, and designing large-scale weaponry for sieges and field engagements. The Greeks developed this kind of big thinking in warfare during the Hellenistic period, while

A Roman soldier's equipment usually included a sword and shield, and sometimes a spear and dagger as well. These weapons were often cheaply made, as they were considered tools of combat rather than works of art.

The Romans paid particular attention to their military forces, not only to defend themselves but also to expand the base of their empire by overtaking smaller, weaker societies. Ancient Roman warriors were considered the most skilled soldiers of their time.

the Romans adapted it in a more streamlined, systematic fashion. Many of the Romans approaches and methods are considered standard practice today. Ordinary weaponry issued to Roman soldiers was manufactured in mass quantities, for relatively little money, and with little care for decoration. Weapons were utilitarian—that is, designed for a specific purpose and nothing more. While it would be an exaggeration to call Roman weapons cheap, their makers were not concerned about creating works of art. Moreover, in keeping with so many of their other practices, Romans did not invent the majority of their military equipment. Instead, they simply adopted the weapons of other societies and modified them to fit their needs. The earliest Roman weapons were modeled after those of the Greeks and the Etruscans—who were among their first adversaries.

A Roman soldier usually carried a shield (called either a *scutum* or a *parma*), a sword (*gladius* or *spatha*), and sometimes a spear (*hasta*) or javelin (*verutum* or *pilum*) for throwing, as well as a dagger (*pugio*) for combat in close quarters. Some soldiers wore a helmet (*galea*) and armor to protect the upper body. There were three main types of armor: chain mail (*lorica hamata*), which featured hundreds of small, interconnected bronze or iron rings; scale armor (*lorica squamata*), which resembled the scales of a reptile; and segmented armor (*lorica segmentata*), which was a kit consisting of several sections that had to be assembled each time the armor was worn. The lorica segmentata featured long, flat strips of metal connected in an overlapping fashion to create separate sheets that covered the lower torso, the upper chest, the back, and the shoulders. Donning, removing, and maintaining the kit was labor intensive, but it provided excellent protection.

Two notable military devices invented by the Romans were the corvus and the caltrop. The corvus was a temporary bridge that could be extended from one ship to another during naval battles. It enabled Roman soldiers to board an enemy vessel quickly. A corvus was usually a wooden plank with guard rails on either side. Rome did not have any significant naval capability during the earliest years of its military development. The only known use of the corvus occurred during the First Punic War against Carthage (264 to 241 BCE). While the corvus was an effective device in ideal conditions, it did not work well in rough waters, as it often caused damage to both vessels.

The caltrop was a more successful, yet startlingly simple, design. A small item of iron or bronze with four spikes, it was designed in such a way that it would always sit on the ground, with three of the four spikes

The caltrop was a simple device invented entirely by Roman military engineers. The sharp spikes were designed to stop advancing soldiers in their tracks, literally.

providing a stable base while the fourth stood with its point upward. Caltrops were very effective in slowing down the movement of enemy troops, both infantry and cavalry, as well as chariots. They were inexpensive to make and could be thrown by the handful and scattered across a road, like jacks.

YESTERDAY AND TODAY

From the building of roads and bridges to the use of reapers during the harvest and the development of an organized and well-equipped military, the ancient Romans made technological strides that still echo throughout modern societies. The Romans were not angelic by any means; they spilled blood and killed thousands of people as they overwhelmed one society after another in their seemingly unquenchable thirst for domination. But we cannot deny that Romans were innovators of the highest order, as they improved the quality of life for their own citizens in ways that proved beneficial to countless humans in the centuries ahead. In this regard, it seems inappropriate to call Roman technology ancient.

circa 753 BCE—Rome is founded, and the monarchic period (when Rome is ruled by kings) begins. Rome is using a lunar calendar based largely on the Greek system.

509 BCE—Tarquinius the Proud, the last of the monarchic kings, is expelled, marking the start of the Roman Republic.

476 BCE—The last of the great Roman emperors, Romulus Augustulus, surrenders his rule, ending over a thousand years of Roman dominance in the region.

410 BCE—The Visigoths sack Rome.

312 BCE—Roman soldiers begin construction on the Via Appia (Appian Way). They also begin work on the first of many major aqueducts.

295 BCE—Romans construct the Minturnae, a bridge along the Via Appia and one of the first to use the stone archways that would become common in Roman bridges.

ca. second century BCE—Romans begin to use pozzolana cement.

ca. first century BCE—Romans are using a water mill at the palace of Cabeira. Romans begin using hypocaustic heating systems and are regularly building insulae.

146 BCE—Rome begins its rule over Greece.

46 BCE—Julius Caesar institutes a new, 365-day calendar with an extra day every four years. It will become known as the Julian calendar.

ca. 27 BCE—Octavian, later called Augustus Caesar, becomes the first Roman emperor, marking the start of the Roman Empire and the end of the Roman Republic.

ca. first century CE—Romans develop the reaping machine.

476 CE—The last Roman emperor, Romulus Augustulus, is removed from power, marking the end of the Roman Empire and the start of the Middle Ages in Europe.

GLOSSARY

aqueduct—A channel, located either above or below ground, designed to keep water continually flowing from one place to another.

arcades—Aqueduct segments that are raised off the ground and usually supported by arches.

arch—The curved top of an opening (like in a doorway or under the span of a bridge), built with blocks that are narrower at the point where they face into the curve.

axle—A long pole or similar shaft extending from the center of a wheel, and from which the wheel rotates.

caltrop—A small, four-spiked metal object designed to sit on the ground with three of the four spikes providing a base while the fourth points upward.

cement— A powder that is made by burning a mixture of clay and limestone.

cistern—A tank for holding and storing water.

corvus—A temporary bridge that extended from one vessel to another during battles at sea.

hypocaust—A system of open spaces through which heat flows from a central furnace for the purpose of heating rooms.

ides—One of three main sections of the early Roman calendar, starting on the night of the full moon; usually the thirteenth or fifteenth of the month.

insulae—Primitive ancient Roman apartment buildings, usually built with inexpensive materials and little attention to detail.

Julian calendar—The calendar created by Julius Caesar in 46 BCE. It featured 365 days per year, with an additional day added to the end of February every four years.

kalends—One of three main sections of the early Roman calendar, marking the period following the first crescent moon after the new moon. Also considered the start of the new month.

limestone—A hard, light gray rock used for building and for making lime.

mansiones—Rest stops along an ancient Roman road.

milia passuum—A Roman unit of measurement for traveling distances, similar to the modern mile. It means "one thousand paces" and is the rough equivalent of 4,860 feet (1.5 km).

mill—A machine used to crush something into smaller pieces between a pair of wheels made of hard, abrasive material, such as stone.

nones—One of three main sections of the early Roman calendar, starting with the moon's first quarter phase; the ninth day before the ides.

pozzolana—A type of volcanic ash that, when mixed with water and lime, forms a particularly powerful cement.

sedimentation tank—A container with a filter used to remove floating, unwanted particles from water.

vallus—A grain-harvesting device that looks similar to a wheelbarrow, with a row of sharp, comblike teeth jutting out from the front.

waterwheel—A large wheel that turns by the force of flowing or falling water.

BOOKS

Brown Reference Group. *Ancient Rome (Cultural Atlas for Young People)*. New York: Chelsea House Publications, 2007.

Deckker, Zilah. *National Geographic Investigates Ancient Rome: Archaeology Unlocks the Secrets of Rome's Past*. Washington, D.C.: National Geographic Children's Books, 2007.

Hinds, Kathryn. *Everyday Life in the Roman Empire*. New York: Marshall Cavendish, 2009.

McCarty, Nick. *Rome: The Great Empire of the Ancient World*. New York: Rosen Publishing, 2008.

Schomp, Virginia. *The Ancient Romans*. New York: Marshall Cavendish, 2008.

Snedden, Robert. *Ancient Rome*. Collingwood, ON: Saunders Book Company, 2009.

WEBSITES

www.historyforkids.org/learn/romans/

The Romans page on the *History for Kids* website. Covers all general aspects of life in ancient Rome, including art, religion, architecture, science, and food. Also has activities and teachers' guides.

---

http://rome.mrdonn.org/

This site is loaded with information and is easily organized into three columns—Rome as a kingdom, a republic, and an empire. Covers many aspects of Roman life.

---

www.socialstudiesforkids.com/subjects/ancientrome.htm

A nicely presented page with links covering slightly offbeat aspects of ancient Rome. It includes a glossary, a discussion of the Twelve Tables system of Roman law, and biographical information about Hannibal, Rome's "greatest enemy."

---

www.kidskonnect.com/content/view/262/27/

The *Kids Konnect* page for ancient Rome covers a broad selection of topics via a simple list of links to other sites dense with information.

INDEX

About the Author

Wil Mara is an award-winning author who has written many educational titles for young readers, covering subjects such as history, geography, animals, social issues, and biographies of notable people. More information about his work can be found at www.wilmara.com.